# HOMEMADE
# DISCIPLES

William Wright, M. Div., Ph. D.

WESTBOW
PRESS®
A DIVISION OF THOMAS NELSON
& ZONDERVAN

WestBow Press books may be ordered through booksellers or by contacting:

WestBow Press
A Division of Thomas Nelson & Zondervan
1663 Liberty Drive
Bloomington, IN 47403
www.westbowpress.com
844-714-3454

ISBN: 978-1-6642-0759-2 (sc)
ISBN: 978-1-6642-0758-5 (e)

Print information available on the last page.

WestBow Press rev. date: 10/27/2020

# DEDICATION

This book is a result of the influence of many men and women of God who have taught me, encouraged me and supported me over the years of my ministry. I was raised in Poughkeepsie N.Y. where almost everyone went to church. My mother, Carrie Mae Edwards, insisted that we all go to church. It was not an option in her house. We attended Second Baptist Church. I received salvation by grace thru faith in the Lord Jesus Christ at Holy Light International Ministries under the leadership of Bishop Addie B. McClinton.

While in Poughkeepsie, I also served under Bishop James Hunt of Bethel Church of God in Christ. My training in ministry began under Bishop Johnnie White Sr. of Hopewell Junction, N.Y. He was my father in ministry who taught to love the Word of God. He also taught me how to love my wife and how to be a husband and father. I am eternally indebted to God for Johnnie White Sr. He adopted me as his spiritual son. I am grateful for Bishop Debra E. Gause, Dr. Jesse V. Bottoms, Bishop Will Palmer, Bishop Wesley T. Cherry Sr. and all of my friends and colleagues in ministry. I am also thankful for my pastor, Dr. John R. Peyton. He saw something special in me. He taught me about the work of the ministry and encouraged me to further my education. I earned a Master of Divinity and a Doctor of Philosophy as a result of his encouragement and influence. I am so grateful for my friend Rev. Millicent West for reading and commenting on my transcript. I am deeply indebted to my sister, Mrs. Veronica Mincey for doing the reading and editing. I wanted my writing to make sense to everyone. I am eternally grateful to my son, Elder Charles C. Stroman 3rd for writing the Forward to the book.

This book is dedicated to my wife, Evangelist Barbara Wright. The woman God gave me to keep me focused and take care of me these many years. I am a blessed man to have such a wonderful wife. All the glory, honor and praise belong to my Lord and Savior Jesus Christ. I owe Him everything!

# CONTENTS

# FOREWORD

Homemade Disciples is an amazing book, not just because my dad wrote it, but because I am a fruit of **Proverbs 22:6 (HCSB)**

**⁶ Teach a youth about the way he should go; even when he is old he will not depart from it.**

First, I would like to tell you that my dad is an amazing man of God. He is a great teacher and a student of the Word. I am so grateful of who God created him to be in my life.

Being the great woman of God that she is, I remember my mother taking me to a Pentecostal church, at the age of six, and I learned a lot about rejoicing loudly. They called it shouting, speaking in tongues, seeing my mother crying and praying. The only thing that was missing was that I didn't get an in-depth teaching of the Bible. When I was nine years old, my mother married my dad. At first, I was apprehensive of the marriage, but dad began to love me and show me something that would help me to be the man I am today. He began to teach by the way he lived. First, I would see him study and read the Word. He was always reading the Bible and studying different sermons and lessons. Then he began to take us to Wednesday night bible studies taught by Dr. Johnnie White, Sr., who was my dad's spiritual father and mentor. Soon he began having family weekly Bible studies. This pattern continued through my adolescent years.

I always viewed my father as a studious teacher of the Word, and he taught me to be the same. I remember he would have me and my younger sisters memorize Scriptures. This practice caused me to become more curious about the Word of God. In my curiosity, I began to read the Bible on my own but did not really have an understanding of what the words meant. So, when I would go to church, I used to clown around and not listen to the sermons being taught by the church's preacher. It seemed so boring to me as it did for most adolescent boys. I would talk to my friends and go to sleep during sermons at church. But through home Bible study, I started to take an interest in the Bible and started to get more understanding. The Word of God and Christianity started to become a part of my everyday life. Then, around 11 years old, I noticed another change happening due to our home Bible studies. While in church, I started to take an interest in the sermons. While my friends were sleeping as soon as the sermons started, I decided that I would start listening to the minister. To my surprise, the church service was not that long. I did not realize that the seeds that were being planted in me were taking hold of my life, developing my Christian journey, and that God was about to bring an increase in my life

Although, of course, I've had my own trials and tribulations throughout my own life and throughout my walk with God, I was always able to lean upon the Word of God that my father instilled in me at a young age. The power of the Word would not let me go! Hallelujah!

Dad taught and instilled in me the best thing a father can give his child, Jesus Christ. I did not know at the time but what he was doing not only changed my life, it also changed the next two generations.

I remember when my first child was born. I knew I wanted to be there for her to teach, pray, and instill God in her heart, and when God blessed me with four more children, I knew I had to get to work at fatherhood. The life lesson of Proverbs 22:6 was passed down to me and I began applying that Scripture to my children. Four of my five children were home schooled and each morning before I went to work, I spent time with them teaching God's word. We would memorize scriptures together. I taught them how to read by reading the Bible. As a family, we went through the whole Bible, chapter by chapter. Of course, it took years to complete. I was determined to give it to them the gift that my dad gave me. We had a lot of fun learning the Bible together and to this day, they still talk about the fun times. Through this important lesson, the opportunity to lead all five of my children to Christ. Their ages are 20, 21, 22, 23, and 29 and Jesus is an important part of all their lives. The oldest is married to a man of God and they have blessed me with a beautiful granddaughter. Guess what she and my son-in-law are doing with my grandbaby? Yes, you guessed it, training her up in the way she should go and when my grandbaby gets older, she will not depart from the Word that has been imparted in her heart. This is truly a legacy that is being passed down through the generations of my family and it can easy be a part of your family as well.

If you have not begun to hold at-home Bible studies, the gems held within this book are a great resource and guide to get a family started as early as today.

Elder Charles C. Stroman, 3rd

# HOMEMADE DISCIPLES INTRODUCTION

Three years ago, I was in a meeting with Northern Virginia District pastors in my role as Virginia State Director of Christian Education for the Full Gospel Baptist Church Fellowship. During the meeting, a pastor asked me a question, "How do we reach the millennials who have left the church?" I thought about the question and my response was not what everyone expected. I said, "you may have to reach millennials the way you reach anyone who does not profess Jesus Christ as Lord and Savior. The problem may be that when they were pre-millennials families and churches did not make them into disciples of Jesus Christ. When they were young, they were not indoctrinated, trained in the things of God." The Scriptures proclaim," **Proverbs 22:6 (HCSB)**

**⁶ Teach a youth about the way he should go; even when he is old he will not depart from it**. The main reason why this book is being written is a result of the millennial question. God gives parents the primary responsibility of discipling their children. This is not something new. In the Old Testament, God told His people of their responsibility to teach, train and indoctrinate their children about their God.

**Deuteronomy 6:4-9 (HCSB)**

⁴ **"Listen, Israel: The Lord our God, the Lord is One.**

⁵ **Love the Lord your God with all your heart, with all your soul, and with all your strength.**

⁶ **These words that I am giving you today are to be in your heart.**

⁷ **Repeat them to your children. Talk about them when you sit in your house and when you walk along the road, when you lie down and when you get up.**

⁸ **Bind them as a sign on your hand and let them be a symbol on your forehead.**

[9] **Write them on the doorposts of your house and on your gates.**

Most parents today are not aware of this responsibility. Our primary intention is to assist parents in fulfilling this responsibility by giving parents practical, doctrinal teaching and lessons on how to disciple their children. In doing so, we will begin to eliminate the millennial problem.

There are many books written on Christian discipleship. Most are a response from the Great Commission given by the Lord Jesus Christ in Matthew 28:18-20:

**Matthew 28:18-20 (HCSB)**

[18] **Then Jesus came near and said to them, "All authority has been given to Me in heaven and on earth.**

[19] **Go, therefore, and make disciples of all nations, baptizing them in the name of the Father and of the Son and of the Holy Spirit,**

[20] **teaching them to observe everything I have commanded you. And remember, I am with you always, to the end of the age."**

Essentially, we are given this command for the purpose of doing two things. First, we are responsible for winning souls. This means that all Christians are called to share the life changing gospel of Jesus Christ. The pastors and leaders in churches have this as their primary responsibility. This call is to witness for Christ with understanding. To do this, one must know what the Good News of the Gospel is all about. Our sharing of the gospel with people who do not know Jesus as Savior and Lord requires us to study the Word of God to obtain the necessary knowledge so we can accomplish what the Lord has commissioned us to do. Secondly, after winning souls, we are tasked with making new converts into disciples of Jesus Christ. That's the simple explanation of the Great Commission.

Finally, the name of this book is called "Homemade Disciples." It is our hope that this book will be used to assist families and churches in fulfilling the Great Commission of winning souls and making disciples with the home as the starting point.

# CHAPTER 1

— — — — — — — — — — — — — — — — — — — — — —

## The Times We Live In

It has been said that we are living in the last days. Some would argue that these are the last of the last days. What can we say about the times in which we live? This is the year 2020. The world is experiencing a pandemic resulting from a plague called the Coronavirus (COVID-19). People are dying all over the world. Men and woman are marrying within the same sex. In the United States homosexuality is considered a normal lifestyle. The commandments of God and the teachings within the Holy Bible are now taken as suggestions. People are living like they will never give an account for the life they are living. The Church of Jesus Christ is teaching little about the consequences of sin or the return of the Lord at the Rapture of the church. In many churches the teaching ministries are focused on prosperity and wealth - not on making disciples. These indeed may be the last days. Our Lord taught on many occasions that there would be a great falling away during the end times. As a result, it should not be surprising that the Lord was asked repeatedly what His disciples should expect during the end times. Here is one of those conversations:

Luke 17:26-30 (HCSB)

26 "Just as it was in the days of Noah, so it will be in the days of the Son of Man:

27 people went on eating, drinking, marrying and giving in marriage until the day Noah boarded the ark, and the flood came and destroyed them all.

28 It will be the same as it was in the days of Lot: people went on eating, drinking, buying, selling, planting, building.

29 But on the day Lot left Sodom, fire and sulfur rained from heaven and destroyed them all.

# WILLIAM WRIGHT, M. DIV., PH. D.

<sup>30</sup> **It will be like that on the day the Son of Man is revealed.**

In verse 26, <sup>26</sup> **"Just as it was in the days of Noah…"** the statement is significant for understanding the times in which we live. Let us look back for a moment for understanding.

**Genesis 6:5-8 (HCSB)**

<sup>5</sup> **When the Lord saw that man's wickedness was widespread on the earth and that every scheme his mind thought of was nothing but evil all the time,**

<sup>6</sup> **the Lord regretted that He had made man on the earth, and He was grieved in His heart.**

<sup>7</sup> **Then the Lord said, "I will wipe off the face of the earth: man, whom I created, together with the animals, creatures that crawl, and birds of the sky—for I regret that I made them."**

<sup>8</sup> **Noah, however, found favor in the eyes of the Lord.**

This is where we are at now! Man has turned his back on God and is doing evil as it was in Noah's day. The only hope for mankind is to repent and receive Jesus Christ as Lord and Savior.

**Proverbs 14:12 (HCSB)**

<sup>12</sup> **There is a way that seems right to a man, but its end is the way to death.**

Man's way has always been different from God's way. The wonderful part of Genesis 6:8 is that Noah found favor with the Lord. That means we still have a chance to change the course of our lives by making the right choices. These are the times in which we live.

In the Book of Revelation, the Apostle John receives a prophecy from the Lord for the seven churches in Asia Minor. These seven churches represent seven periods of time in the history of the Christian church, beginning with Ephesus and ending with Laodicea.

**Revelation 1:10-11 (HCSB)**

<sup>10</sup> **I was in the Spirit on the Lord's day, and I heard behind me a loud voice like a trumpet**

[11] saying, "Write on a scroll what you see and send it to the seven churches: Ephesus, Smyrna, Pergamum, Thyatira, Sardis, Philadelphia, and Laodicea."

Each church was given a word from the Lord about their strengths and weaknesses. They were encouraged by the Lord to make changes to improve their service to Him. The only church that the Lord had nothing good to say about was the Church of Laodicea. Let us read the text together.

**Revelation 3:14-22 (HCSB)**

[14] "To the angel of the church in Laodicea write: "The Amen, the faithful and true Witness, the Originator of God's creation says:

[15] I know your works, that you are neither cold nor hot. I wish that you were cold or hot.

[16] So, because you are lukewarm, and neither hot nor cold, I am going to vomit you out of My mouth.

[17] Because you say, 'I'm rich; I have become wealthy, and need nothing,' and you don't know that you are wretched, pitiful, poor, blind, and naked,

[18] I advise you to buy from Me gold refined in the fire so that you may be rich, and white clothes so that you may be dressed and your shameful nakedness not be exposed, and ointment to spread on your eyes so that you may see.

[19] As many as I love, I rebuke and discipline. So be committed and repent.

[20] Listen! I stand at the door and knock. If anyone hears My voice and opens the door, I will come in to him and have dinner with him, and he with Me.

[21] The victor: I will give him the right to sit with Me on My throne, just as I also won the victory and sat down with My Father on His throne.

[22] "Anyone who has an ear should listen to what the Spirit says to the churches."

In reading this text, what strikes me the most is verse twenty, "[20] **Listen! I stand at the door and knock .**" After reading this verse, I was shocked to hear that the Lord of the church was standing at the door knocking trying to gain access.

The church at Laodicea thought it was rich and wealthy without any needs. It boasted of its prosperity. It suffered primarily from self- sufficiency and self-righteousness. It was a church without the presence of the Lord. The church was neither hot nor cold. There was no passion for Jesus Christ. The Lord called the Laodicean Church lukewarm. He also called it

1. Wretched
2. Miserable
3. Poor
4. Blind
5. Naked

God will not bless a people who are self-absorbed, self-sufficient and self-righteous. He will not bless a church that is not totally dependent upon Him. So, as a result of the arrogance of this church, Jesus said, **16 So, because you are lukewarm, and neither hot nor cold, I am going to vomit you out of My mouth.**

After such a stern rebuke, the Lord then makes a way for this church to find its way back. He says, whatever riches you are seeking after, you need to find in Me. Whatever prosperity you are seeking you can find in the Kingdom of God. He tells the Church of Laodicea that He disciplines those who He loves. He then calls the Church of Laodicea to repentance. To repent means to turn away from what you are doing and to agree with God. In effect, to turn from wickedness to righteousness and obedience.

The church today is a mirrored reflection of the Church of Laodicea. The church in this present age teaches the same blasphemy as the Laodicean Church. The prosperity message is a message that says, God is not enough. What Jesus did on the cross is not enough. We need more than that. God wants all of us to be rich and have no needs. The idea of suffering is directly related to my lack of faith. If I had enough faith, I could call things into existence because I am a little god. I could decree and declare anything I want by using the name of Jesus. This false gospel literally makes the sovereign God and Creator of the universe my personal concierge. I say it and God rushes out to make sure it happens. That is what is called another gospel. The Apostle Paul addressed this kind of teaching in his writings:

**Galatians 1:6-9 (HCSB)**

**6 I am amazed that you are so quickly turning away from Him who called you by the grace of Christ, [and are turning] to a different gospel—**

[7] not that there is another [gospel], but there are some who are troubling you and want to change the gospel of Christ.

[8] But even if we or an angel from heaven should preach to you a gospel other than what we have preached to you, a curse be on him!

[9] As we have said before, I now say again: if anyone preaches to you a gospel contrary to what you received, a curse be on him!

In the mind of Apostle Paul, pursuing any person or thing other than God through the Lord Jesus Christ was pursuing another gospel. The resulting consequence would not be wanted by any human being. Also, the pursuit of riches or pleasurable delights would also be problematic. Paul again deals with this teaching in the text of Scripture:

## 1 Timothy 6:5-10 (HCSB)

[5] and constant disagreement among men whose minds are depraved and deprived of the truth, who imagine that godliness is a way to material gain.

[6] But godliness with contentment is a great gain.

[7] For we brought nothing into the world, and we can take nothing out.

[8] But if we have food and clothing, we will be content with these.

[9] But those who want to be rich fall into temptation, a trap, and many foolish and harmful desires, which plunge people into ruin and destruction.

[10] For the love of money is a root of all kinds of evil, and by craving it, some have wandered away from the faith and pierced themselves with many pains.

There is clearly nothing wrong with having money. Money answers problems for individuals and families. The passion and pursuit of money and riches sometimes leads to "the more I have, the more I want" mentality. Money literally becomes the person's god. Individuals begin to attach spiritual significance to money believing that the more faith you have, the more money you can have.

The dominant message today is the same as the message of the church at Laodicea. The idea of self- sufficiency and the pursuit of wealth and cultural standing has caused many churches today to forget their responsibility. Jesus said the church should be winning souls and making disciples. He said the world would hate the church because it hated Him and that His grace would be with us even in times of trials and suffering. Jesus taught that all sufficiency was found in our relationship with Him:

**Colossians 3:1-4 (HCSB)**

[1] **So if you have been raised with the Messiah, seek what is above, where the Messiah is, seated at the right hand of God.**

[2] **Set your minds on what is above, not on what is on the earth.**

[3] **For you have died, and your life is hidden with the Messiah in God.**

[4] **When the Messiah, who is your life, is revealed, then you also will be revealed with Him in glory.**

The goal of the Christian life is for us to become like Christ. The more mature we become in our faith, the more we can glorify God and show this dying world who Christ is. The Lord is calling for the church to repent. Return to our first love and get back on task. He told the Church at Laodicea and He is telling the church today:

**Revelation 3:19-20 (HCSB)**

[19] **As many as I love, I rebuke and discipline. So be committed and repent.**

[20] **Listen! I stand at the door and knock. If anyone hears My voice and opens the door, I will come in to him and have dinner with him, and he with Me.**

It is time to get back on task. The Lord is standing at the door of our hearts, our homes and our communities bidding us to come and sit with Him. The promise of Jesus is that He will come and receive the church, in the Rapture, to be with Him throughout all of eternity.

**John 14:1-4 (HCSB)**

[1] **"Your heart must not be troubled. Believe in God; believe also in Me.**

² In My Father's house are many dwelling places; if not, I would have told you. I am going away to prepare a place for you.

³ If I go away and prepare a place for you, I will come back and receive you to Myself, so that where I am you may be also.

⁴ You know the way where I am going."

These are the times in which we live!

While we are preparing to make disciples, we must remember our responsibility of winning souls. We call this Evangelism. The souls we win are the persons who are made into disciples of Jesus Christ. Most Christians spend more time at work, among friends and in their communities then they spend at home. I believe that we are all called to share the life changing Gospel of Jesus Christ in the areas that God has placed us. It is no accident that we have the jobs we have and live in the communities we live in. When we are God's Children we are led and directed by His Spirit even when we do not know it. When Jesus called the twelve disciples, they were all engaged in some type of work. Working in the marketplace.

The first words of Jesus to His disciples were "**Matthew 4:19 (HCSB)**

¹⁹ **"Follow Me," He told them, "and I will make you fish for people!"**

His last words before His ascension

**Matthew 28:19-20 (HCSB)**

¹⁹ **Go, therefore, and make disciples of all nations, baptizing them in the name of the Father and of the Son and of the Holy Spirit,**

²⁰ **teaching them to observe everything I have commanded you. And remember, I am with you always, to the end of the age."**

These Scriptures give us our clear mandate to reach as many souls as possible with the Gospel. Since we are planted where we live and work, we must have a strategy for reaching our communities.

## 1 Peter 3:15 (HCSB)

**[15] but set apart the Messiah as Lord in your hearts, and always be ready to give a defense to anyone who asks you for a reason for the hope that is in you.**

To accomplish our evangelistic responsibility, we will need to be familiar with the word of God to share Biblical Truth with others and be ready to give testimony of how the Lord has changed our lives for His Glory. It takes a disciplined time alone with God before we go into the marketplace in order for us to be directed by His Spirit in this work. We must learn to read, study, meditate, memorize and live the word of God. The Lord told his servant Joshua…

## Joshua 1:8-9 (HCSB)

**[8] This book of instruction must not depart from your mouth; you are to recite it day and night, so that you may carefully observe everything written in it. For then you will prosper and succeed in whatever you do.**

**[9] Haven't I commanded you: be strong and courageous? Do not be afraid or discouraged, for the Lord your God is with you wherever you go."**

Hallelujah, this is still true for today. When we saturate ourselves in His word, when we commit to meditate on it day and night and live obediently to His word, when we talk about and discuss the word of the Lord and commit ourselves to the work of God with a strong desire to reach others for the Kingdom of God, He will show Himself strong in us and we will prosper as He has promised. This will require us to get into the Word of God like never before. Especially considering the times in which we live.

## Hebrews 4:12-13 (HCSB)

**[12] For the word of God is living and effective and sharper than any two-edged sword, penetrating as far as to divide soul, spirit, joints, and marrow; it is a judge of the ideas and thoughts of the heart.**

**[13] No creature is hidden from Him, but all things are naked and exposed to the eyes of Him to whom we must give an account.**

When we are studying the word of God, the word of God is studying us. Bringing conviction in our lives and changing us from the inside out. In this way, we are being changed and conforming ourselves to the character and mind of Christ. The combination of the word of God and the work of the Holy Spirit in teaching us and our obedience to the word of God accomplishes the change in our lives.

**Lifestyle Evangelism**

Reverend Dr. John R. Peyton, (this writer's pastor) has said over and over "We can win more to Christ by how we live than by what we say. "We must become visible examples of what it is like to become a devoted follower of Jesus Christ. Other people are watching our life for evidence of a lifestyle that pleases God.

The kind of lifestyle necessary for wining souls is explained by the Paul the Apostle.

**Romans 12:1-2 (HCSB)**

**[1] Therefore, brothers, by the mercies of God, I urge you to present your bodies as a living sacrifice, holy and pleasing to God; this is your spiritual worship.**

**[2] Do not be conformed to this age, but be transformed by the renewing of your mind, so that you may discern what is the good, pleasing, and perfect will of God.**

To effectively win others to Christ, we must have the mind of Christ. We get this mindset through the study, meditation, and application of the Word of God in our lives. This is our spiritual sacrifice and act of worship. We must choose our friends and our opportunities for growth as a priority in life. Our dedication to the plans and purposes of God must be in front of every decision we make. We are called to a holy lifestyle. We no longer live to please the flesh, the world, or the Devil. We live to please God! We are victorious because of our life in Christ.

When we fulfill our roles of going into the world and sharing the gospel with others, there are several methods used in doing our part. Some require pastoral leadership, and some can be family activities. Here are a few for consideration.

In the Local Church

1. Leaders will need to make evangelism a priority and create an atmosphere for winning souls.
2. Prayer evangelism can be established by church prayer ministries. Family, friends, and members of the community can be targeted through prayer. Visitation teams and evangelism ministries can follow up with those who are targeted.
3. Gift evangelism can take place by leaving small gifts on door handles. Gifts can include items like water bottles and gift certificates. In this current pandemic environment, facemasks, cleaning wipes and toilet paper are acceptable gifts. Gifts are good conversation starters leading to conversations about salvation and church membership.
4. Fellowship evangelism can take place by inviting co-workers and neighbors for lunch or any other small gathering.
5. Invitation evangelism can take place through word of mouth or cards which invite persons to church or fellowship.
6. Worship service evangelism takes place when the pastor and ministers preach and teach evangelistically.
7. Servant and Lifestyle evangelism must accompany any other method. Christian lives must reflect the message of Christ.

In the Family

1. Neighborhood evangelism works when relationships are established in communities. Cookouts and servant evangelism are good tools to win souls and show the love of Christ. Family witnessing has always been a great activity to demonstrate the importance of evangelism to children.
2. Prayer evangelism works around the family meal table. Families praying for those who are lost is an effective evangelism tool. Children also learn the importance of evangelism through their participation.
3. Invitation evangelism works well with teens and younger children.

We are living during the times in which creative ways must be put into practice in order to win souls. We are facing a pandemic like we have never seen, and we still need to win souls for Jesus Christ. These are the time in which we live.

# CHAPTER 2

_ _ _ _ _ _ _ _ _ _ _ _ _ _ _ _ _ _ _ _ _ _ _ _

## The Call to Salvation

The Good News – The Gospel of Jesus Christ

The message of the Gospel is simplistic and can be easily understood. When I say that I am saved from my sin, it means the penalty for my sin has already been paid by Jesus Christ on the Cross. Salvation is offered to all who believe in Jesus Christ and what He did for all mankind on the Cross. Salvation is deliverance from sin and its consequences. Jesus Christ paid the penalty for our sin and secured our salvation with eternal life.

**John 3:16-17 (HCSB)**

**16 "For God loved the world in this way: He gave His One and Only Son, so that everyone who believes in Him will not perish but have eternal life.**

**17 For God did not send His Son into the world that He might condemn the world, but that the world might be saved through Him.**

Let me be clear, the Scriptures teach that there is only one way a person can receive salvation and eternal life:

**John 14:6 (HCSB)**

**6 Jesus told him, "I am the way, the truth, and the life. No one comes to the Father except through Me.**

**WILLIAM WRIGHT, M. DIV., PH. D.**

To follow up on this, the Apostle Paul explained this to the Corinthian believers:

**1 Corinthians 15:3-4 (HCSB)**

³ **For I passed on to you as most important what I also received: that Christ died for our sins according to the Scriptures,**

⁴ **that He was buried, that He was raised on the third day according to the Scriptures,**

The clear message is that Christ died for our sins! The only way a person can be lost is if he or she does not accept by faith that which Jesus the Christ has already done. The sin problem is addressed. To miss heaven, one would have to reject God's provision of His Son.

The Great Commission commands us to preach the Good News that Christ died for our sins. Through evangelism, we share what Jesus has done for us and offer salvation to all who would put their faith in Him.

Before I go any further, let me explain the need for salvation because there are lots of people who do not understand all the talk about salvation. The issue of sin and salvation goes all the way back to the Garden of Eden when Adam sinned against God and all of humanity was then separated from God because of the bloodline. Sin brought death just like God promised.

**Genesis 2:15-17 (HCSB)**

¹⁵ **The Lord God took the man and placed him in the garden of Eden to work it and watch over it.**

¹⁶ **And the Lord God commanded the man, "You are free to eat from any tree of the garden,**

¹⁷ **but you must not eat from the tree of the knowledge of good and evil, for on the day you eat from it, you will certainly die."**

Man was created to live forever. All he had to do was be obedient to the command of God. God said, if you do this, the consequence will be death. All human beings became sinners because of Adam's sin. The Apostle Paul explained it this way.

**Romans 5:12 (HCSB)**

¹² Therefore, just as sin entered the world through one man, and death through sin, in this way death spread to all men, because all sinned.

But the story does not end here. The Lord Jesus Christ gave His life for us to obtain our salvation. Again, Salvation is deliverance from sin and its consequences. Salvation is man's only hope. There is no other answer for man's sin. Sinners are saved thru believing and confessing their belief in Jesus Christ.

**Romans 10:9-10 (HCSB)**

⁹ if you confess with your mouth, "Jesus is Lord," and believe in your heart that God raised Him from the dead, you will be saved.

¹⁰ With the heart one believes, resulting in righteousness, and with the mouth one confesses, resulting in salvation.

We are reconciled to God. Brought into right relationship with Him by what Jesus has done for us. We become new creations. Our lives are different. We have become sons and daughters of God when His Spirit takes up residence within us, making us new. The theologians call this regeneration. Spiritually, regeneration means that God brings Christians from being separated from Him by sin to newness of life in Jesus Christ.

**John 3:3 (HCSB)**

³ Jesus replied, "I assure you: Unless someone is born again, he cannot see the kingdom of God."

**2 Corinthians 5:17-19 (HCSB)**

¹⁷ Therefore if anyone is in Christ, there is a new creation; old things have passed away, and look, new things have come.

¹⁸ Now everything is from God, who reconciled us to Himself through Christ and gave us the ministry of reconciliation:

¹⁹ **that is, in Christ, God was reconciling the world to Himself, not counting their trespasses against them, and He has committed the message of reconciliation to us.**

We share the Gospel wherever and whenever possible. In our homes and in the marketplace.

We are not saved by our own merit. There is nothing we can do to save ourselves. The Lord reconciled us to Himself. In doing so He extended His grace towards us by the saving of our souls

**Ephesians 2:8-9 (HCSB)**

⁸ **For by grace you are saved through faith, and this is not from yourselves; it is God's gift—**

⁹ **not from works, so that no one can boast.**

Grace alone thru faith alone. But what is grace?

Grace is unearned favor we receive from God because of God's love for us. We live in a world of earning, deserving, and merit. We are always judged in the world system based upon our ability and achievement. Grace eliminates the judgement. God literally extends unmerited favor on us based upon the life and actions of our Lord Jesus Christ. Only grace makes alive.

A shorthand for grace is - "mercy, not merit." Grace is the opposite of getting what you deserve. Grace is getting the divine favor we do not deserve

Christians live every day by the grace of God. We receive forgiveness according to the riches of God's grace, and grace drives our sanctification. Paul tells us:

**Titus 2:11 (HCSB)**

¹¹ **For the grace of God has appeared, with salvation for all people,**

Spiritual growth does not happen overnight. We have to mature and grow in our relationship with the Lord our Savior. **2 Peter 3:18 (HCSB)**

¹⁸ **But grow in the grace and knowledge of our Lord and Savior Jesus Christ.**

Grace is God's way of telling us how much He loves us. The Lord Jesus Christ is the object of our faith. All of His actions on our behalf proved He is worthy of our worship and our praise. He gets all the glory by extending His grace towards us. We trust Him wholly because of who He is.

What is Faith? Let me share the text with you.

**Hebrews 11:1 (HCSB)**

**¹ Now faith is the reality of what is hoped for, the proof of what is not seen.**

The English word Faith is the Greek word (Pistis). It means persuasion, and complete conviction of the truth without any doubts. The short of it is that the person who has faith completely trusts whatever God says without doubting. It means we do not have to see the results. We trust that God said it and it will most assuredly come to pass. If God's word says Jesus died for our sins. Then Jesus died for our sins. If God says we are saved by grace through faith in what Jesus did for us and not on our own merit. Then it is so. Period.! There is no doubting. If God said it and I never see it, it is still true because God said it.

The Hebrew writer explained faith by giving several testimonies about faith in action. Abel's sacrifice; Enoch's lifestyle and Abraham's obedience. All examples that if we trust completely in what God says he will reward us with eternal salvation. Abraham is considered the father of Faith. Here is how the Apostle Paul explains it.

Grace transforms our desires, motivations, and behavior. Faith assures our complete trust and belief that what God says, He will do.

In fact, our faith in God's grace grounds and empowers everything in the Christian life. Salvation is truly an act of God. Paul explains our road to salvation in his Letter to the Roman Church.

**Romans 4:16-21 (HCSB)**

**¹⁶ This is why the promise is by faith, so that it may be according to grace, to guarantee it to all the descendants—not only to those who are of the law, but also to those who are of Abraham's faith. He is the father of us all**

[17] in God's sight. As it is written: I have made you the father of many nations. He believed in God, who gives life to the dead and calls things into existence that do not exist.

[18] Against hope, with hope he believed, so that he became the father of many nations, according to what had been spoken: So will your descendants be.

[19] He considered his own body to be already dead (since he was about a hundred years old), and the deadness of Sarah's womb, without weakening in the faith.

[20] He did not waver in unbelief at God's promise, but was strengthened in his faith and gave glory to God,

[21] because he was fully convinced that what He had promised He was also able to perform.

Below are the Scriptures traditionally used to explain the way to salvation. We call it Romans Road.

1. **Romans 3:10 (HCSB)**

[10] as it is written: There is no one righteous, not even one;

2. **Romans 3:23 (HCSB)**

[23] For all have sinned and fall short of the glory of God.

3. **Romans 5:12 (HCSB)**

[12] Therefore, just as sin entered the world through one man, and death through sin, in this way death spread to all men, because all sinned.

4. **Romans 6:23 (HCSB)**

[23] For the wages of sin is death, but the gift of God is eternal life in Christ Jesus our Lord.

5. **Romans 5:8-9 (HCSB)**

[8] But God proves His own love for us in that while we were still sinners Christ died for us!

[9] Much more then, since we have now been declared righteous by His blood, we will be saved through Him from wrath.

6.   **Romans 10:9-10 (HCSB)**

[9] if you confess with your mouth, "Jesus is Lord," and believe in your heart that God raised Him from the dead, you will be saved.

[10] With the heart one believes, resulting in righteousness, and with the mouth one confesses, resulting in salvation.

7.   **Romans 10:13 (HCSB)**

[13] For everyone who calls on the name of the Lord will be saved.

# CHAPTER 3

---

## The Call to Discipleship

**Matthew 4:19 (HCSB)**

**¹⁹ "Follow Me," He told them, "and I will make you fish for people!"**

The work of making disciples is what the Lord does when we follow Him fully. He teaches us and molds us into His image and likeness. Our responsibility as followers is to walk in obedience to His word as we learn it and apply the principals within God's word to our lives. The Holy Spirit helps us to grow as our principal teacher. He leads and guides us into all truth according to the Scriptures.

**John 14:26 (HCSB)**

**²⁶ But the Counselor, the Holy Spirit—the Father will send Him in My name—will teach you all things and remind you of everything I have told you.**

Church leaders and parents are intentional in their oversite of the process of helping those under their charge grow into mature Christians.

The term disciple has become a left behind concept in many churches today. If you ask the average Christian about discipleship, they will more that likely point to Peter, James, John, Andrew, and the other disciples mentioned in the Bible. However, the average church goer would not define themselves as disciples of Jesus Christ. Until there is intentional leadership across the spectrum of denominations regarding discipleship, there will not be the conscious effort by members to become true followers of Jesus Christ. Most people are just going to church. Churches are primarily program focused instead of people focused. Discipleship is not a program or a ministry. It is a lifelong commitment to a lifestyle of submitting to Christ and being transformed into His likeness. We become fully devoted followers who are committed to His plans and His purpose for our lives. The following Scriptures emphasize this point.

**Mark 8:34 (HCSB)**

**[34] Summoning the crowd along with His disciples, He said to them, "If anyone wants to be My follower, he must deny himself, take up his cross, and follow Me.**

**Matthew 28:18-20 (HCSB)**

**[18] Then Jesus came near and said to them, "All authority has been given to Me in heaven and on earth.**

**[19] Go, therefore, and make disciples of all nations, baptizing them in the name of the Father and of the Son and of the Holy Spirit,**

**[20] teaching them to observe everything I have commanded you. And remember, I am with you always, to the end of the age."**

What is a disciple?

As previously stated, disciples are those who have the assurance of salvation by grace thru faith in the Lord Jesus Christ and His death on the cross for our sins. Disciples understand the need to grow in grace and in the knowledge of their Lord and Savior Jesus Christ.

Disciples are servants as Jesus pointed out to us,

**Mark 10:45 (NKJV) [45] For even the Son of Man did not come to be served, but to serve, and to give His life a ransom for many."**

Disciples give their time, talent and resources for the furtherance of God's Kingdom.

2 Corinthians 9:6-7 (NKJV) ⁶But this *I say:* He who sows sparingly will also reap sparingly, and he who sows bountifully will also reap bountifully. ⁷*So let* each one *give* as he purposes in his heart, not grudgingly or of necessity; for God loves a cheerful giver.

Disciples are teachable learners.

Acts 17:11 (NKJV) These were more fair-minded than those in Thessalonica, in that they received the word with all readiness, and searched the Scriptures daily *to find out* whether these things were so.

Disciples are accountable.

Hebrews 13:17 (NKJV) Obey those who rule over you, and be submissive, for they watch out for your souls, as those who must give account. Let them do so with joy and not with grief, for that would be unprofitable for you.

Finally, disciples are controlled by the Holy Spirit.

Galatians 5:21-25 (NKJV) ²¹Envy, murders, drunkenness, revelries, and the like; of which I tell you beforehand, just as I also told *you* in time past, that those who practice such things will not inherit the kingdom of God.

²²But the fruit of the Spirit is love, joy, peace, longsuffering, kindness, goodness, faithfulness,

²³gentleness, self-control. Against such there is no law.

²⁴And those *who are* Christ's have crucified the flesh with its passions and desires.

²⁵If we live in the Spirit, let us also walk in the Spirit.

**Home Made Disciples**

We have come to the meat of this discourse. .Let us review the Scriptural mandate for making disciples in the home.

**Deuteronomy 6:4-9(NKJV)**

[4] "Hear, O Israel: The Lord our God, the Lord *is* one!

[5] You shall love the Lord your God with all your heart, with all your soul, and with all your strength.

[6] "And these words which I command you today shall be in your heart.

[7] You shall teach them diligently to your children, and shall talk of them when you sit in your house, when you walk by the way, when you lie down, and when you rise up.

[8] You shall bind them as a sign on your hand, and they shall be as frontlets between your eyes.

[9] You shall write them on the doorposts of your house and on your gates.

**Ephesians 6:4(NKJV)**

[4] And you, fathers, do not provoke your children to wrath, but bring them up in the training and admonition of the Lord.

In the Old Testament the first five books of the Bible were written by Moses. It is called the Pentateuch. Deuteronomy chapter six (6) beginning with verse number four (4) is the Hebrew Shema. This Scripture is recited twice daily affirming the Jewish God as one God with a command to teach the Shema to the children so they can carry on the tradition throughout their generations. For the purposes of this writing please notice in Deuteronomy chapter six the necessity of consistently teaching children about their God. When they walk by the way, sit in the house, lie down, and rise. There is no other way to continue generations of members of the Faith without teaching children about their God. Symbols and signs and warnings will always accompany the teaching.

**Deuteronomy 6:13-15(NKJV)**

[13] You shall fear the Lord your God and serve Him and shall take oaths in His name.

[14] You shall not go after other gods, the gods of the peoples who *are* all around you

<sup>15</sup> **(for the Lord your God** *is* **a jealous God among you), lest the anger of the Lord your God be aroused against you and destroy you from the face of the earth.**

In addition, in **Ephesians 6:4** the Apostle Paul admonishes fathers to **but bring them up**(children) **in the training and admonition of the Lord.**

The questions from Christian parents are "How do we do this? What is the process? How do we get started?

It all starts with making the home an environment for Christian growth. Parents must begin with being totally committed to Christ. Here are some things that you can do first.

# CHAPTER 4

– – – – – – – – – – – – – – – – – – – – – –

## Building a Spiritual House

1.  <u>Make God's word the focus of your existence.</u>

**Joshua 1:8(NKJV)**

**⁸ This Book of the Law shall not depart from your mouth, but you shall meditate in it day and night, that you may observe to do according to all that is written in it. For then you will make your way prosperous, and then you will have good success.**

Memorizing Scripture, talking about the word of God and discussing the meaning of Scripture throughout the day helps children understand the priority of living and learning about God.

**2 Timothy 3:16-17 (NKJV)**

**¹⁶ All Scripture *is* given by inspiration of God, and *is* profitable for doctrine, for reproof, for correction, for instruction in righteousness,**

**¹⁷ that the man of God may be complete, thoroughly equipped for every good work.**

Children must learn that the origin of Scripture is not from man, but from God.

Hebrews 4:12(NKJV)

[12] For the word of God *is* living and powerful, and sharper than any two-edged sword, piercing even to the division of soul and spirit, and of joints and marrow, and is a discerner of the thoughts and intents of the heart.

The only way to build is to allow the wise master builder to build you.

2. <u>Make every effort to build your faith daily.</u>

**Romans 10:17 (NKJV)**

[17] So then faith *comes* by hearing, and hearing by the word of God.

3. <u>Teach your family the word of God</u>

**Proverbs 22:6 (NKJV)**

[6] Train up a child in the way he should go, And when he is old he will not depart from it.

There are so many reasons why we have issues with raising children. Perhaps we have abandoned them and given them over to video games, cell phones, electronic pads and television. They can end up not being reached for Jesus Christ because many parents have not invested the time and energy necessary for the personal and spiritual development of their children. In short, they have been allowed to raise themselves and are greatly influenced by the world around them. Not by what we have done, but by what we did not do. We need to make a commitment to stop the Devil and recapture our children's attention by focusing them on the God who created them and the Lordship of Jesus Christ. Focusing them on a future filled with the joy of the Lord that will strengthen them during the difficult times in which we live. Something that will give them a hope and a future.

4. Make prayer a priority in your house.

**1 Thessalonians 5:17 (NKJV)**

[17] Pray without ceasing.

**Colossians 1:9-11 (NKJV)**

[9] **For this reason we also, since the day we heard it, do not cease to pray for you, and to ask that you may be filled with the knowledge of His will in all wisdom and spiritual understanding;**

[10] **that you may walk worthy of the Lord, fully pleasing *Him,* being fruitful in every good work and increasing in the knowledge of God;**

[11] **strengthened with all might, according to His glorious power, for all patience and longsuffering with joy;**

God has given us responsibility for our families. Our church equips and disciples us and we equip our families. Daily prayer and being God focused is paramount to building a spiritual home. We need to take the focus off us and our personal issues as we seek to accomplish the will God in the earth. It does not matter if you are a single or two parent family. With the assistance of the Holy Spirit and intentional leadership in our churches we are enabled to get the job done.

5.  Strengthen your marriage.

If you are married, strengthen your marriage. Children are greatly influenced by the kind of relationship their mothers and fathers have. If you want your children to have strong relationships that are holy and healthy, you need to have a marriage that is strong and visibly strong in front of your children. If you are not married, there is a need to live a life of commitment to Jesus Christ so your children will know how to live as well.

## Discipling Children

When teaching and training children and making them into disciples of Jesus Christ there are several things you should take into account. First, the children must understand that the emphasis is not on just obtaining knowledge. Your focus is taking what is learned and assisting them in making it a part of their lives through application of the Biblical principles learned through Biblical teaching. In addition, there must be an emphasis on the power of the word of God to change us and help us be obedient to God. Therefore, we will be including Bible memory verses in our lessons.

WILLIAM WRIGHT, M. DIV., PH. D.

**Psalms 119:9-11(NKJV)**

[9] **How can a young man cleanse his way? By taking heed according to Your word.**

[10] **With my whole heart I have sought You; Oh, let me not wander from Your commandments!**
[11] **Your word I have hidden in my heart, That I might not sin against You!**

Second, there must be a time set aside for family Bible Study that is carved in stone and there should be no activity that trumps this set aside time. Sports, shopping, and other extracurricular activities should not have priority over time in God's Word as a family. You are advised to discuss this and pick a time that will not cause priority issues within the family. Third, Bible studies should take no longer than one hour unless there are multiple questions that need to be answered. You will need time to discuss application and to make sure each member of the family knows and understands the memory verse.

## The Role of the Church in Family Discipleship

The pastor of the church provides intentional leadership to the entire congregation. He or she must promote family discipleship within the church. The development of family and youth ministries within the church should be focused on how to support marriages and single parent families as they disciple children in the home. This means, providing materials and training on the use of those materials by the Christian Education Department in the church. It also means providing guidance and direction in selecting family outreach opportunities within a community. The youth minister can also provide support for the discipling of children within the church and can serve as a resource for parents in this regard.

## Critical Christian Doctrines

There are critical Christian doctrines that we need to summarize before we present the lesson plans to begin family Bible study. These are not intended to be detailed. They are simply intended to give each reader a frame of reference as you teach truth within your homes. Please fell free to do more personal study on these doctrines and ask questions from church pastors and leaders.

## The Assurance of Salvation by Grace thru Faith

We discussed this earlier. Let us summarize what we have already said.

**1 John 5:11-13(NKJV)**

[11] And this is the testimony: that God has given us eternal life, and this life is in His Son.

[12] He who has the Son has life; he who does not have the Son of God does not have life.

[13] These things I have written to you who believe in the name of the Son of God, that you may know that you have eternal life, and that you may *continue to* believe in the name of the Son of God.

**John 10:27-30 (NKJV)**

[27] My sheep hear My voice, and I know them, and they follow Me.

[28] And I give them eternal life, and they shall never perish; neither shall anyone snatch them out of My hand.

[29] My Father, who has given *them* to Me, is greater than all; and no one is able to snatch *them* out of My Father's hand.

[30] I and *My* Father are one."

**Ephesians 2:8-10 (NKJV)**

[8] For by grace you have been saved through faith, and that not of yourselves; *it is* the gift of God, [9] not of works, lest anyone should boast.

[10] For we are His workmanship, created in Christ Jesus for good works, which God prepared beforehand that we should walk in them.

## The Trinity

The **Trinity** is a Christian doctrine, stating that <u>God</u> exists as three *persons*, or in the Greek *hypostases*, but is <u>one being</u>. The *persons* are understood to exist as <u>God the Father</u>, <u>God the Son</u> (incarnate as <u>Jesus Christ</u>), and God the <u>Holy Spirit</u>. Here are some supporting Scriptures:


**Matthew 28:19(NKJV)**

[19] Go therefore and make disciples of all the nations, baptizing them in the name of the Father and of the Son and of the Holy Spirit,


**John 1:1-4 (NKJV)**

[1] In the beginning was the Word, and the Word was with God, and the Word was God.

[2] He was in the beginning with God.

[3] All things were made through Him, and without Him nothing was made that was made.

[4] In Him was life, and the life was the light of men.

The Word mentioned in the preceding text is referring to Jesus Christ. Notice verse fourteen (14) of the same chapter.


**John 1:14 (NKJV)**

[14] And the Word became flesh and dwelt among us, and we beheld His glory, the glory as of the only begotten of the Father, full of grace and truth.

Jesus Christ referred to His Father as God.


**John 8:53-54 (NKJV)**

[53] Are You greater than our father Abraham, who is dead? And the prophets are dead. Whom do You make Yourself out to be?"

[54] Jesus answered, "If I honor Myself, My honor is nothing. It is My Father who honors Me, of whom you say that He is your God.

The Holy Spirit is called God in Scripture. Here is an example.

**Acts 5:3-4 (NKJV)**

[3] But Peter said, "Ananias, why has Satan filled your heart to lie to the Holy Spirit and keep back *part* of the price of the land for yourself?

[4] While it remained, was it not your own? And after it was sold, was it not in your own control? Why have you conceived this thing in your heart? You have not lied to men but to God."

Let us answer a few questions regarding the Holy Spirit. Who is the Holy Spirit? Answer, God!

**John 14:16-18 (NKJV)**

[16] And I will pray the Father, and He will give you another Helper, that He may abide with you forever--

[17] the Spirit of truth, whom the world cannot receive, because it neither sees Him nor knows Him; but you know Him, for He dwells with you and will be in you.

[18] I will not leave you orphans; I will come to you.

What are some of the roles of the Holy Spirit?

**John 14:26 (NKJV)**

[26] But the Helper, the Holy Spirit, whom the Father will send in My name, He will teach you all things, and bring to your remembrance all things that I said to you. John 16:12-14

[12] I still have many things to say to you, but you cannot bear *them* now.

¹³ However, when He, the Spirit of truth, has come, He will guide you into all truth; for He will not speak on His own *authority,* but whatever He hears He will speak; and He will tell you things to come.

¹⁴ He will glorify Me, for He will take of what is Mine and declare *it* to you.

How do I receive the Holy Spirit?

**John 1:12 (NKJV) But as many as received Him, to them He gave the right to become children of God, to those who believe in His name: (Galatians 4:6) And because you are sons, God has sent forth the Spirit of His Son into your hearts, crying out, "Abba, Father!"**

You receive the Holy Spirit when you are converted. When you are born again and receive salvation the Holy Spirit takes up residence within you. What are some of the character traits of those who are indwelt by the Holy Spirit?

**Galatians 5:22 (NKJV) ²²But the fruit of the Spirit is love, joy, peace, longsuffering, kindness, goodness, faithfulness, ²³ gentleness, self-control. Against such there is no law.**

We are admonished by the Apostle Paul to be filled with the Spirit.

**Ephesians 5:18 (NKJV) ¹⁸And do not be drunk with wine, in which is dissipation; but be filled with the Spirit,**

To illustrate, if we drank water from a glass, then the water would be inside us. However, if we went to the beach and stepped into the ocean, then we would be in the water. We receive, as it were, a drink of the Holy Spirit when we are saved, but when we are filled with the Spirit, it is as if that initial drink becomes an ocean that completely surrounds us.

Just as the indwelling Spirit that Christians receive when they are saved reproduces the life of Jesus, so the outpoured, or filling of the Spirit reproduces the ministry of Jesus within us.

Why Do We Need to be filled with Holy Spirit?

We need a power beyond ourselves for service and ministry in Christ's Kingdom. When Jesus gave the Great Commission (Matthew 28:19-20), He knew that His disciples could not fulfill it in their own power. Therefore, He had a special gift in store for them: It was His plan to give them the same power that He had — the power of the Spirit of God.

**Here are some keys to having a good home Bible Study:**

- Have a family meeting and discuss what night and time of the week would be best to have the study.
- Stick to the time that is agreed upon and start and finish on time!
- Make a decision that this will be a family priority.
- Start with a prayer.
- Give each family member an opportunity to share what was learned from last weeks lesson. Have them recite the Memory Verse. Post the memory verse on the children's bedroom doors and the refrigerator.
- Always remember what the purpose of this study is…

  1. To develop a closer relationship with God.
  2. To develop a closer relationship with each other.
  3. To unite as a Godly family.
  4. Strengthen God's Church by making disciples.

- End with a prayer.

# CHAPTER 5

- - - - - - - - - - - - - - - - - - -

## Home Bible Study Keys and Lesson Outlines

# LESSON #1

– – – – – – – – – – – – – – – – – –

## God's Families

**OBJECTIVE:** To read and discuss what God says about Christian families.

**Scriptures for study:**

Genesis 2:21-24

Deuteronomy 6:4-9

**Family Discussion:**

- Who were the first man and woman?
- How was Eve created?
- Why was Eve created?
- In Genesis 2:24, how is a family started?
- Looking at Deuteronomy 6:4-9…
- How much should we love God? (vs. 5)
- Where should we hold God's commandments? (vs. 6)
- Whose responsibility is it to teach children about God? (vs. 7)
- How often should we talk about and teach God's commands? (vs. 7, 8, 9)
- Can you as a family make a commitment to begin talking about God as a family more?

**Challenge:** Take time to discuss your family's favorite verses in the Bible. Decide on a "theme" verse for your family. Have someone copy it or type it on a piece of paper. Place the verse in several locations throughout the house to remind you of your family's commitment to God.

**Memory Verse: Deuteronomy 6:5 (NKJV)**

[5] **You shall love the Lord your God with all your heart, with all your soul, and with all your strength.**

# LESSON #2

- - - - - - - - - - - - - - - - - - - - - - - - - - -

## God's Plan for Children & Parents

**OBJECTIVE:** To read and discuss what God says about the relationship between

parents and children.

**Scriptures for study:**

Deuteronomy 5:16

Ephesians 6:1-4

**Family Discussion:**

- Children, who are you to obey? (Eph. 6:1)
- Why are you to obey your parents? (6:1)
- In verse 2, Paul writes to "Honor" your father and mother. What does honor mean?

*Special esteem or respect – The American Heritage Dictionary*

- This was the first commandment with what? (6:2)
- What was the promise? (6:3)
- Fathers, to what should you not provoke your children? (6:4)
- How should parents bring up their children? (6:4)
- In training a child there must be teaching. What are ways a parent can teach their children?

**Concluding thoughts:** This passage has beautiful balance. Children are to obey their parents, and parents are to treat their children in such a way that the children will want to obey.

**Challenge:** Take time to have the children list some things that demonstrate their parents' love for them. Parents please take some time to share some things that you feel are admirable qualities in your children. What are some areas that the family needs to improve in? Conclude with a prayer asking God to help your family grow in respecting and loving each other more.

**Memory verse: Ephesians 6:1(NKJV)**

[1] **Children, obey your parents in the Lord, for this is right.**

# LESSON #3

— — — — — — — — — — — — — — — — — — — — —

## Patience

**OBJECTIVE:** To read and discuss what God says about patience.

**Scriptures for study:**

Genesis 12:1-5, then 17:15-17, then 21:1-3 (Abraham's patience)

Ephesians 4:2

1 Thessalonians 5:14-15

**Family Discussion:**

- What promises did God make to Abraham when he was 75 years old?
- How old was Abraham when his son, Isaac, was finally born?
- So, how long did Abraham have to wait for God's promise to start coming true?
- God promised to make Abraham's family into a great nation. How long do you think it took for that promise to come true? (days? Months? Years? Centuries?)
- Read what Hebrews 6:13-15 says about Abraham!
- Next time you have to wait awhile for something to happen, what can you do to make the waiting easier? Discuss some examples.
- Sometimes, to have patience means to wait for something to happen, like Abraham did. Other times, to have patience means to be tolerant of other people. What does
- Ephesians 4:2 and 1 Thessalonians 5:14-15 mean? Think of some situations when it is hard to be patient with a family member. How can you show patience to your family?
- Remember, patience is a Fruit of the Spirit.

**Challenge:**

A proverb is a wise saying. Read these two proverbs about patience: Proverbs 14:29 and 16:32. Now let each family member make up his or her own wise saying about patience.

**Memory verse: Isaiah 40:31(NKJV)**

[31] **But they that wait upon the LORD shall renew** *their* **strength; they shall mount up with wings as eagles; they shall run, and not be weary;** *and* **they shall walk, and not faint.**

# LESSON #4

– – – – – – – – – – – – – – – – – – – – – – – –

## Kindness

**OBJECTIVE:** To read and discuss what God says about kindness.

**Scriptures for study:**

Mark 2:1-12 (the kindness of 4 friends)

Matthew 25:31-46

**Family Discussion:**

- In the story in Mark 2, how did the friends of the paralyzed man show kindness?
- What might have happened to the paralyzed man if his friends had not helped him get to Jesus?
- How did Jesus show kindness to the paralyzed man? (2 ways)
- In Matthew 25, Jesus explains that when we do something kind for another person, we are also showing kindness to whom?
- If Jesus were in the hospital, would you go visit him? If Jesus were hungry, would you give him something to eat? Of course, you would. When you think of people who are in need, picture Jesus in that situation. It may make it easier to show kindness!
- Discuss Proverbs 14:21 and verse 31. Think of some ways your family can show kindness to needy people. Plan a project!
- What is the opposite of kindness? Read Ephesians 4:31 and 32 to find out how families should treat each other and how they should NOT treat each other.

WILLIAM WRIGHT, M. DIV., PH. D.

## Challenge:

Each family member should do at least one random act of kindness tomorrow. Think of a way to be helpful to someone, or surprise somebody with an act of love! Keep your idea a secret until it is done, then tomorrow night, tell each other about your experience. How does it make you feel to be kind to others?

**Memory verse: Ephesians 4:32(NKJV)**

[32] **And be kind to one another, tenderhearted, forgiving one another, just as God in Christ forgave you.**

# LESSON #5

‒ ‒ ‒ ‒ ‒ ‒ ‒ ‒ ‒ ‒ ‒ ‒ ‒ ‒ ‒ ‒ ‒ ‒

## Being Thankful

**OBJECTIVE:** To read and discuss what God says about being thankful.

**Scriptures for study:**

Luke 17:11-19; Leviticus 13:45-46;1 Thessalonians 5:18; Luke 9:16;Philippians 4:6

**Family Discussion:**

- What did the Law of Moses command lepers to do? (Leviticus 13:45-46) How would you have felt if you had leprosy and had to live as an outcast?
- How many lepers came to Jesus? What did they want?
- Jesus told the lepers to go and show themselves to the priest. What happened as they went on their way?
- How many of the men remembered to say thank you? What did Jesus say to the man who came back? (verses 17-19)
- Under what circumstances should we give thanks to God? Read 1 Thessalonians 5:18.
- Read Luke 9:16. What did Jesus always do before eating a meal? Does your family remember to thank God before each meal?
- Many times when we pray, we are asking for things. What should we remember to do when God answers our prayers? How do you tell God thank you? Discuss Philippians 4:6.

**Challenge:**

Count your blessings. Have each family member tell 5 things they are thankful for.

**Memory verse: 1 Thessalonians 5:18(NKJV)**

[18] **in everything give thanks; for this is the will of God in Christ Jesus for you.**

# LESSON #6

— — — — — — — — — — — — — — — — — — —

## Being Responsible

**OBJECTIVE:** To read and discuss what God says about being responsible.

**Scriptures for study:**

Daniel 6:1-23; Colossians 3:22-24;1 Thessalonians 4:11-12

**Family Discussion:**

- What responsibilities did King Darius give to Daniel? (verses 1-2)
- Did Daniel do a good job? How do you know? (verse 3)
- Some men were jealous of Daniel and wanted to get him in trouble with the king, but they could not find anything wrong with his work. Why couldn't they find fault with Daniel? (verse 4)
- Daniel was not corrupt or negligent. That means that he didn't steal from the king (he could be trusted), and he didn't neglect to do what he was told. Was Daniel was a responsible person? Are you?
- Being responsible means being trustworthy. When Daniel was thrown into the lions' den, did Daniel find out that God was trustworthy? Was God the one who was responsible for saving Daniel's life?
- Read the verses in Colossians. They are about how slaves should be responsible even when their masters are not watching. How could this same principle apply to you when you are working at school or at your job? How could it apply to children when their parents give them chores to do?

**Challenge:**

List the responsibilities that each family member has at home. What can each of you do to be more responsible? Who is always watching?

**Memory verse: Colossians 3:23(NKJV)**

[23] **And whatever you do, do it heartily, as to the Lord and not to men,**

# LESSON #7

- - - - - - - - - - - - - - - - - - - - - - - - - -

## Respecting Others

**OBJECTIVE:** To read and discuss what God says about respecting others.

**Scriptures for study:**

1 Samuel, chapter 26; Luke 6:31;1 Peter 2:17 and Romans 12:10

**Family Discussion:**

- King Saul tried many times to kill David. Then one day, David had the chance to get revenge. He could have killed Saul while Saul was sleeping. But, what did
- David do instead? David showed respect to King Saul. Did Saul deserve it? Why do you think David showed him respect anyway?
- What did King Saul do when he found out that David had spared his life? (verse 21) Children—Tell about ways you can show respect to these people: parents, grandparents, teachers, policemen, the elders.
- Parents—Share ways you can show respect to these people: (Husband/wife, children, neighbors, employer, the elders).
- Why do you think Luke 6:31 is called "the golden rule?" How can this verse help you to show respect to others?
- Do you think it is a command from God that you should respect other people?
- Read 1 Peter 2:17 and Romans 12:10 to find out!

**Challenge:**

This week show respect for each other. Listen with interest when someone is telling you about his or her day. Pick up your own messes. Don't aggravate each other. Treat everyone else the way YOU want to be treated!

**Memory verse: Luke 6:31(NKJV)**

[31] **And just as you want men to do to you, you also do to them likewise.**

# LESSON #8

— — — — — — — — — — — — — — — — — — — — — — —

## Sharing

**OBJECTIVE:** To read and discuss what God says about sharing.

**Scriptures for study:**

John 6:1-13; Romans 12:13; Hebrews 13:16; Acts 4:32-35

**Family Discussion:**

- Why was there a crowd of people following Jesus? What did Jesus ask Philip?
- What did Philip reply? What food did Andrew find among the people? Whose lunch was it? What did Jesus do with his lunch?
- How many people were fed because the little boy shared his lunch? Did everyone get enough to eat? How much food was left over?
- Can you make dinner-for-one become enough food to feed more than 5,000 people? Why not? How was Jesus able to do it?
- What does Romans 12:13 say about sharing? How does God feel when we share with others, according to Hebrews 13:16?
- When the church began, the believers were united like one big happy family. What did they do, according to Acts 4:32? The next verses tell us that there were no needy persons among them. Why not?
- What else can you share besides material things? Your time? Your love? What else? The best thing of all that anyone can share is the good news of Jesus Christ!

**Challenge:**

Discuss some ways that your family can share with others. Plan a sharing project, such as giving some of your clothes to an organization that helps the needy. Maybe you could donate cans of food, as well. Can you think of other ways to share?

**Memory verse: Hebrews 13:16(NKJV)**

[16] **But do not forget to do good and to share, for with such sacrifices God is well pleased.**

# LESSON #9

- - - - - - - - - - - - - - - - - - -

## Self-Control

**OBJECTIVE:** To read and discuss what God says about self-control.

**Scriptures for study:**

Matthew 26:57-67 and 27:19-31; Psalms 106:3; Romans 12:17-18; Titus 2:11-12

**Family Discussion:**

- What bad things did the Jews and Romans do to Jesus? List as many as you can remember. (Reread the story if you need to.)
- When the Jews slapped Jesus and hit him with their fists, did Jesus go into a rage?
- When Jesus was flogged, did he curse at anyone? When the soldiers dressed Jesus up like a king and made fun of him, did Jesus fight them? When the soldier's spit on him, did he spit on them, too? Did Jesus have self-control?
- How do you think God feels about people who practice self-control? Read Psalms 106:3. Blessed is he who does right…how often?
- When someone makes you mad, what is the wrong thing to do? What is the best thing to do? Read Romans 12:17-18
- When you are tempted to do wrong, how can you have self-control? Find out by reading Titus 2:11-12.
- Do you like to be punished? The best way to avoid punishment is to do what is right! Discipline yourself! Remember self-control means YOU be in charge of YOU!

**Challenge:**

Have you seen the bracelets that say "WWJD?" It means "What Would Jesus Do?" The story you read today reminds you that Jesus had excellent self-control. This week, every time you are tempted to do something wrong, or to get angry, remember to ask yourself that question. Then do what Jesus would do if he were in that situation!

**Memory verse: Psalms 106:3 (NKJV)**

³ **Blessed *are* those who keep justice, *And* he who does righteousness at all times!**

# LESSON #10

– – – – – – – – – – – – – – – – – – – – – – – –

## Telling the Truth

**OBJECTIVE:** To read and discuss what God says about telling the truth.

**Scriptures for study:**

Acts 4:32 through 5:11; Revelation 21:8; Proverbs 12:22

**Family Discussion:**

- What happened to Ananias when he told a lie? What happened to Sapphira when she lied, too?
- If Ananias and Sapphira had told the truth about how much money they kept from the sale of the land, and how much they were giving to the church, how would this story have been different?
- Why do you think verse 11 says, "Great fear seized the whole church and all who heard about these events"?
- Who always knows when you are lying? What does God say in Revelation 21:8 about liars?
- Read Proverbs 12:22. How does God feel about lying? How does he feel about people who are honest?
- Jesus had a saying that is repeated over and over in the New Testament. Find out what it was by reading Matthew 18:3, Luke 21:3, and Luke 23:43. Do you think
- Jesus always told the truth? Why?

**Challenge:**

Imagine what would happen if no one ever told the truth. Could you believe your history teacher? Would you trust your doctor? What if an air traffic controller lied to a pilot about a clear runway? Think of some more examples. Why is it so important to always tell the truth?

**Memory verse: Proverbs 12:22(NKJV)**

[22] **Lying lips** *are* **an abomination to the Lord, But those who deal truthfully** *are* **His delight.**

# LESSON #11

— — — — — — — — — — — — — — — — — — — — — —

## Forgiveness

**OBJECTIVE:** To read and discuss what God says about forgiveness.

**Scriptures for study:**

Genesis 45:1-15 and 50:15-21

Romans 12:17-21; Leviticus 19:18 and Colossians 3:13

**Family Discussion:**

Joseph's brothers sold him into slavery. They told Joseph's father that an animal had killed him. Joseph was a slave in Egypt, even spending time in prison for a crime he didn't commit. But God was with Joseph. Years later, God used him to save people from a famine (even his own brothers). Read what happened when the brothers found out that Joseph was the ruler in charge of famine relief! (45:1-15)

- Did Joseph forgive his brothers? What did he do to prove that he forgave his brothers for what they had done? (50:15-21)
- Joseph was a powerful ruler in Egypt. He could have locked his brothers away in a prison for the rest of their lives, or even had them killed! Why do you think Joseph chose not to get revenge? (50:19, 20)
- What does the Bible say about revenge? Discuss Romans 12:17-21.
- When you choose not to forgive someone you are "holding a grudge." Is it a sin to hold a grudge? Discuss Leviticus 19:18.

- When it seems hard to forgive someone, think about Jesus dying on the cross to forgive sins. Think of what he endured…
- He did that to forgive YOU of YOUR sins! Is it too much for him to ask you to forgive others? Think about Colossians 3:13.

**Challenge:**

Try carrying a brick around with you for awhile. Think of the brick as a grudge that you have against someone. The brick will become heavy and burdensome. Eventually, it will be a relief to get rid of it. The point is: Don't carry a grudge…it's not worth it!

**Memory verse: Colossians 3:13(NKJV)**

[13] **bearing with one another, and forgiving one another, if anyone has a complaint against another; even as Christ forgave you, so you also** *must do.*

# LESSON #12

‒ ‒ ‒ ‒ ‒ ‒ ‒ ‒ ‒ ‒ ‒ ‒ ‒ ‒ ‒ ‒ ‒ ‒ ‒

## Saying "I'm Sorry"

**OBJECTIVE:** To learn the importance of saying, "I'm sorry."

**Scriptures for study:**

Jonah, chapters 1 and 2; James 5:16;1 John 1:8-10; Luke 18:9-14

**Family Discussion:**

- What did God tell Jonah to do? What did Jonah do instead?
- Jonah knew he was guilty of disobeying God. When the storm arose, the sailors asked Jonah what he had done to make his God angry. Did Jonah blame it on someone else, did he tell a lie, or did he admit that it was his fault? (verse12)
- Jonah told the sailors to throw him into the sea. When they did, what happened to the sea? Then what happened to Jonah?
- What did Jonah do while he was inside the fish? (2:1) Do you think God forgave Jonah? Why do you think so?
- What should you do when you have committed a sin: Blame it on someone else?
- Lie about it? Say you are sorry and stop doing wrong?
- How does the Bible instruct us to say "I'm sorry?" Read and discuss James 5:16 and 1 John 1:8-10.
- Saying "I'm sorry" is very important, but it is also important to stop doing what you did wrong. Some people are only sorry that they got caught. Some are truly sorry enough to repent. How can you tell the difference?

**Challenge:**

Compare the attitudes of the two men in the story found in Luke 18:9-14. Who had the right attitude? How does this story apply to you?

**Memory verse: James 5:16(NKJV)**

[16] Confess *your* faults one to another, and pray one for another, that ye may be healed. The effectual fervent prayer of a righteous man availeth much.

# LESSON #13

- - - - - - - - - - - - - - - - - - - -

# Obeying Authority

**OBJECTIVE:** To read and discuss what God says about obeying authority.

**Scriptures for study:**

Genesis 6:5 through 7:5; Romans 13:1-5;1 Peter 2:13-14;Ephesians 5:22-28 and 6:1-2.

**Family Discussion:**

- God gave Noah specific instructions. What did God want Noah to build? Did he expect Noah to build it a certain way? What did God tell Noah to take into the ark?
- Which people were allowed to enter it?
- Did Noah obey God's authority? Quote Genesis 6:22. What do you think would have happened if Noah had disobeyed God?
- Only Noah and his family were saved. What happened to everyone else on earth (the ones who were disobedient to God)?
- God has authority over every person. We must obey him. God also expects us to obey other people who have authority over us. Read the verses listed above from
- Romans and 1 Peter. Name all the people whom you must obey. (parents, boss, teacher, police, etc.)
- Why do we have to have rules? Imagine what this country would be like if there were no laws at all. What would school be like if there were no rules?
- What are God's rules for families? Read and discuss Ephesians 5:22-28 and 6:1-2.

**Challenge:**

What are your family's rules? Discuss why those rules are necessary. What are the consequences of disobeying the rules? What are the benefits of obeying the rules?

**Memory verse: Hebrews 13:17(NKJV)**

[17] Obey them that have the rule over you, and submit yourselves: for they watch for your souls, as they that must give account, that they may do it with joy, and not with grief: for that *is* unprofitable for you.

# LESSON #14

— — — — — — — — — — — — — — — — — — — —

## Salvation by Grace

**OBJECTIVE:** To read and discuss what God says about Salvation by Grace

**Scriptures for study:**

Ephesians 2:8,9

John 3:16

Romans 8:35-39

**Family Discussion:**

- How are we saved?
- Who is Jesus Christ?
- Can I do anything to save myself?
- Can I lose my salvation?

**Challenge:** Ask a family member to practice witnessing to a sibling or to you while you are discussing salvation by grace through faith.

**Memory Verse: Ephesians 2:8-9 (NKJV)**

**8 For by grace you have been saved through faith, and that not of yourselves; *it is* the gift of God, 9 not of works, lest anyone should boast.**

# LESSON #15

— — — — — — — — — — — — — — — — — — —

## Holiness

**OBJECTIVE:** To read and discuss what God says about living a holy life.

**Scriptures for study:**

Romans 6:16-19

Hebrews 12:14

Romans 7:18-20

**Family Discussion:**

- What is the meaning of living holy?
- What can we do as individuals to live holy?
- How does prayer and Bible Study play a part in helping me to live holy?

**Challenge:** Have family members discuss a person in the Bible who lived a holy life.

**Memory Verse: Hebrews 12:14 (NKJV)**

[14] Pursue peace with all *people,* and holiness, without which no one will see the Lord:

# LESSON #16

— — — — — — — — — — — — — — — — — — — — —

## Sexual Purity

**OBJECTIVE:** To read and discuss what the Bible says about sexual purity

**Scriptures for study:**

1 Corinthians 6:13-20

**Family Discussion:**

- What is sexual purity? Explain Abstinence to your children.
- What does the Bible mean by "my body is the Temple of the Holy Spirit"?
- What are some of the ways I can win this battle in my life?

**Challenge:** Discuss, "True Love Waits" with the family members. Discuss the benefits of living a life of sexual purity. Challenge each member of the family to make a commitment to live sexually pure.

**Memory Verse: 1 Corinthians 6:19 (NKJV)**

**¹⁹ Or do you not know that your body is the temple of the Holy Spirit *who is* in you, whom you have from God, and you are not your own?**

Please note that there is a program called "True Love Waits" that church youth pastor can use as a resource to help families teach sexual purity for pre-teens and teenagers. The True Love Waits pledge states: "Believing that true love waits, I make a commitment to God, myself, my family, my friends, my future mate and my future children to be sexually abstinent from this day until the day I enter a biblical marriage relationship." In addition, they promote sexual purity, which encompasses not only abstaining from intercourse before marriage, but also abstaining from sexual thoughts, sexual touching, pornography, and actions that are known to lead to sexual arousal." Information about "True Love Waits" can be obtained by contacting Lifeway Christian Resources.

# LESSON #17

– – – – – – – – – – – – – – – – – – – –

## The Fruit of the Spirit

**OBJECTIVE:** To read and discuss what God says about the Fruit of the Spirit.

**Scriptures for study:** Galatians 5:22-26, Ephesians 5:9

**Family Discussion:**

- Discuss each one of the Fruit of the Spirit.
  Love, joy, peace, longsuffering, kindness, goodness, faithfulness, gentleness, self-control
- What is the most difficult part of living a fruitful life?
- Explain and discuss longsuffering.
- Explain and discuss why these are fruit and not fruits of the Spirit.

**Challenge**

Why are Fruit of the Spirit important for living a Christian life that is pleasing to God.

**Memory verse: Galatians 5:22-23 (NKJV)**

²² **But the fruit of the Spirit is love, joy, peace, longsuffering, kindness, goodness, faithfulness,**
²³ **gentleness, self-control. Against such there is no law.**

# LESSON #18

- - - - - - - - - - - - - - - - - - - - - - - -

## Biblical Faith

**OBJECTIVE:** To read and discuss Biblical Faith

**Scriptures for study:** Hebrews 11, James 1:2-8, 2Corinthians 7:7, Galatians 2:16-20, Mark 11:21,22

**Family Discussion:**

- Discuss the definition of Biblical Faith.
- What does Abraham have to do with faith?
- How does faith operate in the life of the believer in Jesus Christ
- Explain how we are saved by grace thru faith.
- Explain what faith has to do with our life of prayer.

**Challenge**

What does Jesus Christ have to do with faith? Talk about it until the family understands this question.

**Memory verse: Hebrews 11:1-3 (NKJV)**

**¹ Now faith is the substance of things hoped for, the evidence of things not seen.**

**² For by it the elders obtained a *good* testimony.**

[3] By faith we understand that the worlds were framed by the word of God, so that the things which are seen were not made of things which are visible.

The following are activities parents can do with their children to help in the discipleship training.

**Suggestions for Family Projects**

- Memorize the books of the New Testament.
- Memorize the books of the Old Testament.
- Develop an outreach of service that you and your family can do.
  - Write cards to the shut-ins, widows or widowers.
  - Write notes of appreciation to your Bible class teachers.
  - Rake someone's yard.
  - Put together a care package for someone in need.
- Memorize I Corinthians 13.
- Memorize the 12 Apostles.
- Memorize the 23rd Psalm.
- Memorize the 12 sons of Jacob.
- Memorize the verses that teach us the plan of salvation. (Roman's Road)

Christian families are also the best place for teaching spiritual disciplines. Spiritual disciplines are practiced in a Christians life to help them mature and build a closer relationship to the Lord Jesus Christ. The disciplines also help build Christian character and strengthen the faith of the believer in Christ. Finally, spiritual disciplines do an inward work in the person practicing them and show a mature, positive witness to observers of how to practice living the Christian life. Spiritual Disciplines include prayer, fasting, meditation, study and giving.

# CHAPTER 6

— — — — — — — — — — — — — — — — — —

## Spiritual Disciplines

The Christian family is the ideal place to learn and practice spiritual disciplines. For the purposes of this chapter, we will be discussing four disciplines that we practice. We will also discuss how to teach them to your children. The disciplines we will be discussing are prayer and fasting, meditation, study and giving.

# PRAYER AND FASTING

— — — — — — — — — — — — — — — — — — — — — —

**Colossians 1:9-14 (NKJV)**

[9] For this reason we also, since the day we heard it, do not cease to pray for you, and to ask that you may be filled with the knowledge of His will in all wisdom and spiritual understanding;

[10] that you may walk worthy of the Lord, fully pleasing *Him*, being fruitful in every good work and increasing in the knowledge of God;

[11] strengthened with all might, according to His glorious power, for all patience and longsuffering with joy; [12] giving thanks to the Father who has qualified us to be partakers of the inheritance of the saints in the light. [13] He has delivered us from the power of darkness and conveyed *us* into the kingdom of the Son of His love, [14] in whom we have redemption through His blood, the forgiveness of sins.

Paul's prayer for the Colossian Church in which they would:

1) Understand God's will- **Purpose**

2) Be impacted by spiritual wisdom- **Practice**

3) Be joyful to endure hardship-**Patience**

4) Recognize their relationship to God-**Privilege**

Through this prayer we immediately recognize that the primary purpose of prayer is to accomplish the will of God in the earth. This intercessory prayer gives us direction on how we should pray for others. All prayer surrounds the idea that we are called to be workers together with God to accomplish His will. We are often trapped in the idea of calling out to God for what He has already promised. In doing so, we minimize our effectiveness in prayer. How do we pray? Let us look at the teaching of Jesus on this subject.

**Matthew 6:5-13 (NKJV)**

[5] **"And when you pray, you shall not be like the hypocrites. For they love to pray standing in the synagogues and on the corners of the streets, that they may be seen by men. Assuredly, I say to you, they have their reward.**

[6] **But you, when you pray, go into your room, and when you have shut your door, pray to your Father who *is* in the secret *place;* and your Father who sees in secret will reward you openly.**

[7] **And when you pray, do not use vain repetitions as the heathen *do*. For they think that they will be heard for their many words.**

[8] **Therefore do not be like them. For your Father knows the things you have need of before you ask Him.**

[9] **In this manner, therefore, pray: Our Father in heaven, Hallowed be Your name.**

[10] **Your kingdom come. Your will be done On earth as *it is* in heaven.**

[11] **Give us this day our daily bread.**

[12] **And forgive us our debts, As we forgive our debtors.**

[13] **And do not lead us into temptation, But deliver us from the evil one. For Yours is the kingdom and the power and the glory forever. Amen.**

This is called the model prayer. When we first learn it, we recite it verbatim. However, as we grow in our Christian walk, we begin understanding how to pray. When teaching this to children, be sure to emphasize the various parts of this model prayer.

First, notice that we enter into God's presence by addressing Him as Our Father. Immediately we see that there is a relationship between us and our God. God has invited us into His Holy presence.

**Hebrews 4:14-16 (NKJV)**

¹⁴ **Seeing then that we have a great high priest, that is passed into the heavens, Jesus the Son of God, let us hold fast *our* profession.** ¹⁵ **For we have not an high priest which cannot be touched with the feeling of our infirmities; but was in all points tempted like as *we are, yet* without sin.** ¹⁶ **Let us therefore come boldly unto the throne of grace, that we may obtain mercy, and find grace to help in time of need.**

We come into the presence of our God boldly with the expectation of finding grace and help. According to the model prayer, we come secretly and privately into His presence knowing that we will be rewarded openly.

**Psalms 100:4-5 (NKJV)**

⁴ **Enter into His gates with thanksgiving, *And* into His courts with praise. Be thankful to Him, *and* bless His name.** The reason for this action on our part is because of the next verse. ⁵ **For the Lord *is* good; His mercy *is* everlasting, And His truth *endures* to all generations.**

We come into His presence with an attitude of worship. We cry out to Him, "**Hallowed be Your name.**" In other words, your name is Holy. It is the name above every name. We follow by saying our true purpose of coming to Him. It does not matter the gravity of the situation or the complexity of the issue. In the model prayer we see that the priority is always

**"Your kingdom come. Your will be done on earth as *it is* in heaven."**

We know that no situation can be resolved the right way unless God's will is done in the answer to the prayer. It eliminates our propensity to have selfish intentions. We want God's Kingdom to come and His will to be done so we can continue to enjoy His bountiful blessings. This is why Paul wrote this to the Colossian church,

**Colossians 3:1-2 (NKJV)**

¹ **If then you were raised with Christ, seek those things which are above, where Christ is, sitting at the right hand of God.** ² **Set your mind on things above, not on things on the earth.**

One of the reasons this was written was that when we communicate with our heavenly Father, we come with the right understanding and determination of accomplishing His Will in the Earth because our mindset will be right. In this we recognize the need to pray for others. We petition the Lord for our families, friends, country, lost souls, marriages, spiritual and secular leaders, and humanity in general that all will come to salvation and deliverance. **"Give us this day our daily bread"** is not just talking about physical need for food and substance. Our daily bread also includes our spiritual need for His Word.

**Jeremiah 15:16 (NKJV)**

[16] **Your words were found, and I ate them, And Your word was to me the joy and rejoicing of my heart; For I am called by Your name, O Lord God of hosts.**

**Luke 4:4 (NKJV)**

[4] **But Jesus answered him, saying, "It is written,** *'Man shall not live by bread alone, but by every word of God.'"*

In this model prayer, we can take all our needs to the Lord. It does not matter if they are physical, spiritual, or psychological. We always pray and ask even though He knows what we need before we ask.

**Matthew 6:8 (NKJV)**

[8] **... For your Father knows the things you have need of before you ask Him.** We begin with worship and after petitioning the Lord for our needs and the needs of others we go back to worship and praise.

[12] **And forgive us our debts, As we forgive our debtors.**

We ask for forgiveness of sin. When we are born again believers we praise and thank God for the forgiveness of sins and that our names are written in the Book of Life. We then pray for His guidance and direction in our lives.

**[13] And do not lead us into temptation But deliver us from the evil one.** The Holy Spirit will lead us in the way of righteousness and keep us focused on the Lord. He will show us what Paul teaches in his first Epistle to the Corinthians.

**2 Corinthians 10:2-5 (KJV)**

**[2] But I beseech *you*, that I may not be bold when I am present with that confidence, wherewith I think to be bold against some, which think of us as if we walked according to the flesh. [3] For though we walk in the flesh, we do not war after the flesh:**

**[4] (For the weapons of our warfare *are* not carnal, but mighty through God to the pulling down of strong holds;) [5] Casting down imaginations, and every high thing that exalteth itself against the knowledge of God, and bringing into captivity every thought to the obedience of Christ;**

He ends the model prayer with praise and the acknowledgement of the sovereignty of God.

**For Yours is the kingdom and the power and the glory forever. Amen.**

Finally, we ask every prayer in the name of Jesus Christ our Lord.

**John 16:23-24(NKJV)**

**[23] And in that day you will ask Me nothing. Most assuredly, I say to you, whatever you ask the Father in My name He will give you.**

**[24] Until now you have asked nothing in My name. Ask, and you will receive, that your joy may be full.**

# FASTING

— — — — — — — — — — — — — — — — — — — — —

Fasting is when you decide to let go of physical food in order to receive nourishment from the spiritual world. For a period, you deny your physical desires to focus on your spiritual desires.

Fasting does not impress God. It cannot manipulate God or prove any level of spiritual ability on your part. It simply allows you to eliminate any obstacles as you seek the face of God for answers and direction in your life. Fasting will help you listen more attentively to God

**Isaiah 58:6 (NKJV)**

⁶ *"Is* **this not the fast that I have chosen: To loose the bonds of wickedness, To undo the heavy burdens, To let the oppressed go free, And that you break every yoke?**

Throughout the history of the world, many fasts were called by leaders to point the people's hearts towards God. Fasting breaks down our human dependence on the physical world and directs us to God, who is almighty. In this we find the answer to life's most difficult problems. Always remember that when you are fasting you will get hungry. The spiritual food of God's word and the determination to do the will of God will provide the needed nourishment. Jesus pointed that out while talking with His disciples.

**John 4:31-34 (NKJV)**

³¹ **In the meantime His disciples urged Him, saying, "Rabbi, eat."**

³² **But He said to them, "I have food to eat of which you do not know."**

³³ **Therefore the disciples said to one another, "Has anyone brought Him *anything* to eat?"**

[34] Jesus said to them, "My food is to do the will of Him who sent Me, and to finish His work.

Fasting and prayer is sometimes necessary when dealing with demonic activity which require focus and concentration.

## Matthew 17:14-21 (NKJV)

[14] And when they had come to the multitude, a man came to Him, kneeling down to Him and saying,

[15] "Lord, have mercy on my son, for he is an epileptic and suffers severely; for he often falls into the fire and often into the water.

[16] So I brought him to Your disciples, but they could not cure him."

[17] Then Jesus answered and said, "O faithless and perverse generation, how long shall I be with you? How long shall I bear with you? Bring him here to Me."

[18] And Jesus rebuked the demon, and it came out of him; and the child was cured from that very hour.

[19] Then the disciples came to Jesus privately and said, "Why could we not cast it out?"

[20] So Jesus said to them, "Because of your unbelief; for assuredly, I say to you, if you have faith as a mustard seed, you will say to this mountain, 'Move from here to there,' and it will move; and nothing will be impossible for you.

[21] However, this kind does not go out except by prayer and fasting." Clearly, there are times in which we will necessarily need to fast and pray.

# MEDITATION

— — — — — — — — — — — — — — — — — — — — — — —

**Psalms 1:1-2 (NKJV)**

[1] Blessed *is* the man Who walks not in the counsel of the ungodly, Nor stands in the path of sinners, Nor sits in the seat of the scornful;

[2] But his delight *is* in the law of the Lord, And in His law he meditates day and night.

**Joshua 1:8 (NKJV)**

[8] This Book of the Law shall not depart from your mouth, but you shall meditate in it day and night, that you may observe to do according to all that is written in it. For then you will make your way prosperous, and then you will have good success.

The word meditation comes from the Latin word meditārī. Meditating on Scripture is the process of focusing on a specific Bible passage and reflecting on it's meaning and application. For example, if I meditate on the 23rd Psalm beginning with the first verse.

**Psalms 23:1 (NKJV)**

**The Lord *is* my shepherd; I shall not want**

I would begin to think about who the Lord is to me. He is my shepherd. I would then begin to focus on what a shepherd does. How he takes care of the sheep. Protects the sheep. Provides for the sheep. I can then ponder on how much God loves me and how good God has been to me. He Lords over me like a shepherd lords over the sheep. It will cause me to love Him more. I would follow Him more fully. Do you get the point? Here is another example.

**WILLIAM WRIGHT, M. DIV., PH. D.**

**Psalms 119:9-12 (NKJV)**

[9] How can a young man cleanse his way? By taking heed according to Your word.

[10] With my whole heart I have sought You; Oh, let me not wander from Your commandments!
[11] Your word I have hidden in my heart, That I might not sin against You!

[12] Blessed *are* You, O Lord! Teach me Your statutes!

When I begin to meditate on this text of Scripture, I immediately see that by seeking the Lord and putting His word in my heart gets the needed result of refraining from living a life of sin. Memorizing it and meditating on the word of God allows me to hide it in my heart and keep His commandments. It is important to begin meditating on single verses of Scripture and then graduate to paragraphs and chapters. Meditation leads to more obedience to God's word because during meditation the Scriptures are internalized.

# STUDY

— — — — — — — — — — — — — — — — — — — — — — — —

The discipline of study is very important to any person's development as a disciple of Jesus Christ. To properly understand the word of God a disciple must learn the Inductive Study Method of looking at a text of Scripture.

Inductive Bible study consists of three component parts, which we will look at separately, but which frequently overlap in practice. These three parts are observation, interpretation, and application.

**Observation answers the question: What does the passage say?** Observation is the foundation that must be laid if you want to accurately interpret and properly apply God's Word.

Observation requires time and practice because it helps determine what the passage is saying. You will discover that the more you read and get to know a book of the Bible, the more its truths will become obvious to you.

**Interpretation answers the question: What does the passage mean?** The basis for accurate interpretation is always careful observation. Interpretation is the process of discovering what the passage means. As you carefully observe Scripture, the meaning will become apparent. However, if you rush into interpretation without accurate observation, your understanding will be guided by what you think, what you feel, or what other people have said, rather than what God's Word says.

Interpretation can also involve separate actions or steps that go beyond merely observing the immediate text. Sometimes you have to look at other references. However, always let Scripture interpret Scripture. You may also use other helps, such as word studies or resources such as commentaries and Bible dictionaries to check your conclusions or to supplement your understanding of the historical or cultural setting of the text.

**Application answers the question: How does the meaning of this passage apply to me?** This is the first thing we want to know when we read the Bible. Once you know what a passage means, you are not only responsible for putting it into practice in your own life, but accountable if you don't! Ultimately, then, the goal of personal Bible study is a transformed life and a deep and abiding relationship with Jesus Christ.

Application takes place as you are confronted with truth and decide to respond in obedience to that truth. The basis for application is **2 Timothy 3:16-17 (NKJV)"All Scripture is inspired by God and profitable for teaching, for reproof, for correction, for training in righteousness; so that the man of God may be adequate, equipped for every good work."**

When you know what God says, what He means, and how to put His truths into practice, you will be equipped for every circumstance of life. To be equipped for every good work of life—totally prepared to handle every situation in a way that honors God—is not only possible, it is God's will.

# GIVING

----

I am especially concerned that what is said here today is understood by all of us because God's word says that above all we should get understanding. Our principle launching scripture is found in **1 Corinthians 4:1-2 (NKJV):**

**¹Let a man so account of us, as of the ministers of Christ, and stewards of the mysteries of God.**

**² Moreover it is required in stewards, that a man be found faithful.**

Our primary responsibility before God is to be faithful. We need to be faithful because the very nature of stewardship is that God is the owner and we are managers over what He has entrusted to our hands.

**Psalm 24:1 (NKJV) The earth is the LORD'S, and the fulness thereof; the world, and they that dwell therein.**

**I want to talk about money. I know many Christians want to know what their responsibility is in giving under this covenant we have in Christ.** The Law was given by Moses, but grace and truth came by Jesus Christ. The Hebrew writer says in chapter eight and verse six that Jesus Christ is the mediator of a better covenant established on better promises. Amen


**Scripture References**

**Proverbs 3:9-10 (NKJV)**

**9 Honour the LORD with thy substance, and with the firstfruits of all thine increase:**

**10 So shall thy barns be filled with plenty, and thy presses shall burst out with new wine.**

WILLIAM WRIGHT, M. DIV., PH. D.

**Malachi 3:8-10 (NKJV)**

⁸ "Will a man rob God? Yet you have robbed Me! But you say, 'In what way have we robbed You?' In tithes and offerings.

⁹ You are cursed with a curse, For you have robbed Me, *Even* this whole nation.

¹⁰ Bring all the tithes into the storehouse, That there may be food in My house, And try Me now in this," Says the Lord of hosts, "If I will not open for you the windows of heaven And pour out for you *such* blessing That *there will* not *be room* enough *to receive it.*

**2 Corinthians 9:6-8 (NKJV)**

⁶ But this *I say:* He who sows sparingly will also reap sparingly, and he who sows bountifully will also reap bountifully.

⁷ *So let* each one *give* as he purposes in his heart, not grudgingly or of necessity; for God loves a cheerful giver.

⁸ And God *is* able to make all grace abound toward you, that you, always having all sufficiency in all *things,* may have an abundance for every good work.

Some churches have used the Scriptures to promote an atmosphere of fear when it comes to giving in the church. On Sundays, we open our time of giving by asking the fear question, **" Will a man rob God?"** and then pronounce God's judgment, **"you are cursed with a curse."** This powerful language can pierce a person's heart and cause spiritual distress. The true fact is that tithing was an act of worship in which the person tithing did at least **three things**:

**First**, the person giving acknowledged the first commandment that you shall have no other God's before me. Since man's love of money is the root or cause of most of man's evil, tithing prioritized a person's life by having the person honor the Lord with his or her giving and thereby showing that all of creation belonged to God. It was an act of worship on the part of the person giving.

**Second**, tithing under the law was designed for the purpose of supporting the redemptive plan of God by enabling the priest's under Aaron's priesthood to do at least two major things. First, to have financial support for their families. Also, the priests purchased the sacrificial animals and elements necessary for the performance of their duties in the temple. The sacrifices were necessary because the people's sins would not have been covered without sacrifice.

**Third**, the tithe was also used to help support the poor.

I was convinced that our giving in the new covenant was never tithing because in my view the New Testament did not teach tithing. This is a serious pastoral issue because the way a pastor teaches this can determine how his or her congregation receives favor and blessings from God. It can affect a family's income as well as the outcome of a business or the prosperity of a church because giving is worship.

The issue of a Christian being cursed has been dealt with at the cross by our Lord Jesus Christ. There are no cursed Christians! Christians are blessed with every spiritual blessing in Christ Jesus.

**Ephesians 1:3 (NKJV)**

³ **Blessed** *be* **the God and Father of our Lord Jesus Christ, who has blessed us with every spiritual blessing in the heavenly** *places* **in Christ,**

**Galatians 3:13-14 (NKJV)**

¹³ **Christ has redeemed us from the curse of the law, having become a curse for us (for it is written,** *"Cursed is everyone who hangs on a tree"***),**

¹⁴ **that the blessing of Abraham might come upon the Gentiles in Christ Jesus, that we might receive the promise of the Spirit through faith.**

While we are a blessed people, we still must follow the leading of the Lord in giving in order to prosper. Let us take a quick look back at Proverbs.

**Proverbs 3:9-10 (NKJV)**

⁹ **Honor the Lord with your possessions, And with the firstfruits of all your increase;**

¹⁰ **So your barns will be filled with plenty, And your vats will overflow with new wine.**

The above Scripture proclaims that we honor the Lord with our possessions. The King James Version says our "substance".

1. Our giving honors God: it is an act of worship.
2. God is to receive the first fruits of our increase.

When we give to God as he prescribes, we have promises.

1. We will not have lack.
2. Our blessing will overflow.

First fruit giving simply means God gets the first offering before bills and other obligations are taken care of. It is the recognition that God is first in a person's life and He provides all we have.

Additionally, we are asked to give to those who are teaching and ministering to them.

**Galatians 6:6 (NKJV)**

**⁶ Let him who is taught the word share in all good things with him who teaches.**

**1 Corinthians 9:13-14 (NKJV)**

**¹³ Do you not know that those who minister the holy things eat *of the things* of the temple, and those who serve at the altar partake of *the offerings of* the altar?**

**¹⁴ Even so the Lord has commanded that those who preach the gospel should live from the gospel.**

Clearly, pastors and other ministry workers should be supported by the people for whom they are ministers. Our first fruit offering is the tithe because it represents our worship to the Lord our God who created all things and holds all things together by power of His own will. He challenges us in try Him and see if He will not open the windows of heaven and pour out blessings, we will not have room enough to receive. The first fruit or the tithe is giving begins. It belongs to the Lord. His law is now written in our hearts and we give like Abraham gave, cheerfully, not grudgingly or of necessity. We give because of who He is. Also, we give because we love the Lord and we want to sow bountifully into His kingdom.

The rest of our giving is our time and talent for the work of the kingdom. This will increase as we grow in grace and in the knowledge of our Lord and Savior Jesus Christ.

When teaching children about giving we can practice giving tithes and offerings in their presence. Secondly, we can ask them to begin practicing giving from their allowance or monies they earn from chores.

# CLOSING REMARKS

Making disciples is work. Parents sign on for the work when they bring children in this world. The beautiful thing is that they do not have to do it alone. There are five separate and distinct persons involved in the process of making disciples. The Lord God, the Holy Spirit, the parents, the church, and the children. When all four work together in unity, the result is dynamic disciples who follow the Lord fully devoted to Him.

The Lord works inside of our children, transforming them into His likeness and giving them the full assurance of salvation. He moves them from glory to glory. His word becomes the food for our very existence. Every promise the Lord makes to us is fulfilled in us as we study His word and obey the precepts and demands found in the word of God. Our prayer and devotional lives improve as our faith is increased because of the word of God. His Spirit superintends the process teaching us what we need to know and challenges us to move forward in our walk with Him.

Parents prepare and teach the children about the Lord from their early stages of human development. Family Bible studies and Christian activities reinforce our faith and gives us the ability to grow in grace and in the knowledge of our Lord and Savior Jesus Christ. The parental example of living the Christian faith shows children how to live out what is learned in the Scriptures. In this effort, parents and children grow together in their relationship to the Lord and to one another. Faith continues to the next generation.

The church supports the parent's responsibility by discipling them and equipping them to do what the Lord has assigned for them as the people who are primarily responsible for the discipling of children. Pastors and youth ministers support wherever is needed in solving and explaining biblical issues for parents when they have questions.

Children follow the admonition of scripture by obeying and submitting to the parent's authority to train them up in the way they should go. They should complete all assignments and participate in all spiritual activities as directed by their parents. When they do, they will increase their quality of life and be made into disciples of Jesus Christ with the full benefits of joy and peace in the Holy Spirit.

This is our hope for families, that all would become fully devoted followers of Jesus Christ. That each member would find their place in God's Kingdom and flourish. That they all become disciples who will one day make disciples.

We have included evangelism, basic church doctrine and church disciplines in this book giving parents additional tools to work with. The Bible study lessons, and memory verses are designed to keep the focus on God and His way of living. Our prayer is that you will take advantage of all resources and seek additional help from pastors and youth ministers to complete the assignment of making children into dynamic, homemade disciples of Jesus Christ.

William T. Wright, M.Div., Ph.D.

President, John 8:32 Ministries

# ABOUT THE AUTHOR

Dr. William Wright is a fully devoted follower of Jesus Christ. He is a pastor/teacher who understands the necessity of beginning Christian Discipleship in the home. He has taught at various churches, conferences, and seminars about making disciples, marriage enrichment and church growth.

Dr. Wright is the founding pastor of Emmanuel Bible Fellowship, Dumfries, VA, Chaplain for the Dumfries VA Police Department, President of John 8:32 Ministries and Virginia State Director of Christian Education for the Full Gospel Baptist Church Fellowship of Virginia. He holds a BA in Political Science from Marist College, Poughkeepsie, N.Y., a M.Div. from Andersonville Baptist Seminary, Camilla, Ga. and a PhD in Christian Education from Faith Bible College and Seminary, Temple Hills, Md.

Pastor Wright enjoys spending time with his wife Barbara. He also enjoys watching N.Y. sports teams, training local ministry leaders, and swimming for personal exercise. He and his wife have three children, Charles, Tambra and Starr. They have nine grandchildren and one great grandchild. Dr. Wright is a native of Poughkeepsie, N.Y. He currently resides in Northern Virginia.

Printed in the United States
By Bookmasters